A BRIEF HISTORY OF QUEEN ELIZABETH II

Duty, Diplomacy, and Decades on the Throne: Navigating a Changing World

SCOTT MATTHEWS

Contents

"I have to be seen to be believed."

- Queen Elizabeth II

Introduction

In modern history, few figures stand as vividly or command as much reverence as Queen Elizabeth II. A symbol of continuity in an age of change, her reign spanned over seven decades, a period marked by profound transformations both within the United Kingdom and across the globe. *A Brief History of Queen Elizabeth II* embarks on an exploration of the life and legacy of one of the world's most iconic monarchs, a woman who wore the crown with unparalleled grace, resilience, and an unwavering sense of duty.

From the vibrant streets of post-war Britain to the digital age's global stage, this book covers the journey of a young princess who ascended the throne at a tender age and grew to become the matriarch of not only a nation but an entire Commonwealth of nations. Her story is one of personal sacrifices, public service, and the subtle art of diplomacy, which she wielded with both a mother's touch and a stateswoman's acumen.

Yet, beyond the grandeur of state occasions and the weighty affairs of state, Elizabeth II's reign was punctuated with moments of profound humanity—her quiet humor, her love for her family, and her connection with people from all walks of life. These moments, often overlooked, are what truly defined her as a monarch for the ages.

As we peel back the layers of her extraordinary life, I invite you on a journey not just through the history books, but into the heart of a queen who, in bridging tradition and progress, became a legend in her own right. Through pivotal moments and personal anecdotes, this book seeks to capture the essence of Queen Elizabeth II's reign, offering a unique glimpse into the life of a woman who, in steering the monarchy into the 21st century, left behind a legacy as enduring as the crown she bore with such dignity.

So, whether you're a royal enthusiast, a history buff, or simply fascinated by the story of a remarkable life lived at the helm of one of the world's oldest institutions, *A Brief History of Queen Elizabeth* promises a captivating journey through the life of a queen who was not just a figurehead, but a beacon of stability, compassion, and inspiration for generations. Let's turn the pages and discover the woman behind the crown, whose legacy will undoubtedly echo through the pages of history.

PART I
A Princess Prepares (1926-1952)

A Childhood Unveiled

On April 21, 1926, at 2:40 am, a baby girl was born to the Duke and Duchess of York, later known as King George VI and Queen Elizabeth, in the heart of London. The joyous event took place at their home at seventeen Bruton Street.

They named their daughter Elizabeth Alexandra Mary, as a tribute to three generations of women in their family: "Elizabeth" after her mother, the Duchess of York; "Alexandra" after her great-grandmother, Queen Alexandra; and "Mary" in honor of her grandmother, Queen Mary.

Her birth was significant enough to be attended by the Home Secretary, following a tradition that Queen Elizabeth would later eliminate.

Due to concerns about the crowds from The General Strike,[1] the baby Elizabeth was often taken out for her daily strolls through a back exit to keep the outings discreet.

In her early years, Princess Elizabeth lived at 145 Piccadilly, a London residence selected by her parents shortly after her birth, and White Lodge in Richmond Park.She also spent time at the homes of her maternal grandparents, the Earl and Countess of Strathmore, including Glamis Castle in Scotland and St. Paul's Walden Bury in Hertfordshire. Additionally, she visited the homes of her paternal grandparents, King George V and Queen Mary, such as Windsor Castle, Balmoral Castle, and Sandringham House.

At just fourteen months old, the Queen made her debut on Buckingham Palace's balcony, cradled by her mother and grandmother, Queen Mary. This occasion was notable as it was the first public instance of Queen Mary being seen holding a child.

At the age of six, she became the youngest homeowner in Britain when she received a unique gift from the people of Wales: a small house (known as a Wendy house) located in the grounds of Windsor's Royal Lodge. This quaint house was named Y Bwthyn Bach, which translates to 'The Little Cottage' in English.

---

[1] The General Strike in the UK, which took place in 1926, was a major industrial action that lasted nine days, from May 3 to May 12. It was called by the Trades Union Congress (TUC) in an attempt to prevent wage reductions and deteriorating working conditions for coal miners, but quickly expanded to include workers from many other industries. The strike is considered one

of the largest acts of collective action in British history, involving over 1.5 million workers across various sectors, including transport, steel making, and printing, among others.

Growing up, Elizabeth had a close bond with her younger sister, Princess Margaret, who was born in 1930. Born four years apart, they shared a world filled with laughter, play, and the unique challenges of royal life. The bond between them was not just of sisters but of best friends, a relationship that would endure the test of time and the weight of crowns.

Elizabeth's education was unconventional. She did not attend a school like other children and was home-tutored along with her sister, like many wealthy female children of the time. Her studies included history, language, literature, and music and were overlooked by her mother and her governess, Marion Crawford (Crawfie).

Crawfie, as she was fondly called, made it her mission to introduce the young girls to life beyond the 'glass curtain' by engaging with the local people during their outings around Balmoral. Despite being in her twenties, Crawfie was chosen by their father for her youthful vigor, a contrast to the elderly relatives the Duke of York grew up with. Her father appreciated Crawfie's ability to actively participate in his daughters' playtime.

Away from formal education, Elizabeth's passion for horses blossomed at the tender age of three, fostered by rides across the royal properties with her father. Moreover, her special connection with corgis began in 1933 when the first family corgi, Dookie, was introduced. This bond was further strengthened when she received a corgi as a gift from her father on her eighteenth birthday. Elizabeth cherished her early years in the countryside, especially her time in Scotland, and enjoyed a vibrant social life with her cousins and extended family members.

A pivotal moment in Elizabeth's early life came in 1936, known as the year of the Three Kings. Her grandfather, King George V, passed away, whom she affectionately used to call "Grandpa England." After the death of her grandfather, her uncle, King Edward VIII, ascended to the throne. However, later that year, Edward VIII abdicated to marry Wallis Simpson, an American divorcee. This abdication thrust Elizabeth's father onto the throne, making her the heir presumptive.[2]

Following her father's ascension to the throne in 1936, the shift in the royal landscape dramatically altered Elizabeth's life. The once carefree days at Bruton Street were replaced with a rigorous schedule of lessons, public appearances, and constitutional studies. Elizabeth began focusing on constitutional history and law to prepare for her eventual role. Her education in these areas included lessons from her father and Henry Marten, the Vice-Provost[3] of Eton.

Additionally, she received religious education from the Archbishop of Canterbury. Princess Elizabeth also enhanced her language skills by learning French, taught by various French and Belgian governesses.

---

[2] "Heir presumptive" refers to a person who is first in line to inherit a throne, title, or estate, but whose claim can be displaced if a more direct heir is born. Unlike an "heir apparent," whose right to the inheritance is absolute and cannot be set aside by the birth of another heir, the position of an heir presumptive is conditional.

[3] In the context of educational institutions in England, particularly in universities, the title "Vice-Provost" typically refers to a senior administrative officer who ranks just below the Provost or Principal of the college or university. The specific duties and responsibilities of a Vice-Provost can vary widely between institutions, but generally, they involve overseeing certain academic or administrative areas, such as academic affairs, research, student services, or faculty relations.

This linguistic proficiency proved to be particularly beneficial for her, especially during visits to French-speaking regions of Canada and countries where French is widely spoken.

Soon, Elizabeth's world, which had already changed due to her father's ascension, underwent another transformation with the looming threat of World War II becoming a reality.

Wartime Duty

As World War II engulfed the world in 1939, Princess Elizabeth's life transformed significantly, and the mere thirteen year old had to witness extreme chaos and violence in the world. During the war, the royal family faced a dilemma: to stay in Britain amidst the dangers or to evacuate to a safer location. Choosing to stay, they became symbols of resilience and defiance against the adversity facing their nation. Elizabeth and Margaret were moved to Windsor Castle for safety, but the King and Queen stayed in Buckingham Palace. During these years, Elizabeth saw the impact of leadership and the importance of standing with the people during hard times.

At Windsor Castle, the princesses helped with the war effort by putting on Christmas plays. The money raised from these plays was used to buy wool, which was then knitted into clothes for soldiers. In 1940, when Elizabeth was fourteen years old, she spoke on the radio for the first time. She talked to other children who had been moved to safer places because of the war. Elizabeth said that they were all trying to help the soldiers and deal with the war's challenges. She believed that everything would turn out okay in the end.

By 1943, Elizabeth was taking on more responsibilities. She made her first public appearance alone when she visited the Grenadier Guards, a military group she was connected to. As she neared eighteen, the government made a special law. It allowed her to help run the country if her father, the King, was sick or out of the country. This happened when he went to Italy in 1944.

In 1945, Elizabeth joined the Auxiliary Territorial Service, a part of the army. She learned how to drive and fix vehicles. Elizabeth was enrolled as a second subaltern, equivalent to a second lieutenant, and later promoted to the rank of junior commander, similar to a captain. Her service number was 230873. She underwent a six-week auto mechanic training course at Aldershot, one of the largest British Army garrisons. Her training included learning to drive and maintain vehicles, a remarkable skill set for a royal princess at that time. She wore a standard ATS uniform, making no concessions for her royal status, which was a powerful statement of gender equality and commitment to stand shoulder to shoulder with her subjects in time of need. Her duties involved not just driving but also the maintenance and repair of vehicles. She learned how to change wheels, deconstruct and rebuild engines, and drive ambulances and other military trucks. Elizabeth's service in the ATS was a practical contribution to the war effort and a symbolic gesture of solidarity with the British people.

The war years also brought Elizabeth closer to her father. She learned a great deal from him about what it meant to serve and lead a nation during a crisis. Her mother, known for her poise and strength, was another strong influence, teaching Elizabeth the importance of duty and public service.

Meanwhile, King George VI and Queen Elizabeth (the Queen Mother) became symbols of national determination. They visited bombed areas in London and other parts of the country, boosting morale and exemplifying the spirit of perseverance. Elizabeth was deeply influenced by her parents' resolve, learning the importance of presence and empathy in leadership. The King's speeches, particularly during the Blitz (a period of intense bombing campaigns by Nazi Germany over Britain in World War II) were instrumental in maintaining public morale. Elizabeth saw firsthand the power of words and the responsibility of leadership during crisis times.

The royal family's decision to stay in London, despite the risks, was a significant morale booster for the British people. Their home, Buckingham Palace, was bombed several times, a stark reminder of the shared dangers of war.

Elizabeth's public appearances and wartime broadcasts played a crucial role in her development as a future monarch. These experiences honed her communication skills and deepened her understanding of the British public's struggles and hopes.

On the day when the war in Europe ended, Elizabeth and Margaret went out secretly into the streets of London to join the celebrations, which the Late Queen later reminisced in a rare interview: "We asked my parents if we could go out and see for ourselves. I remember we were terrified of being recognized... I remember lines of unknown people linking arms and walking down Whitehall, all of us just swept along on a tide of happiness and relief."

At the end of the war in 1945, Elizabeth emerged not just as a princess but also as a young woman who had shared in the trials and tribulations of her nation. Her time in the ATS, public appearances, and broadcasts during the war were more than just royal duties; they were the forging of a monarch who would lead with experience, empathy, and a deep connection to her people.

A Royal Romance

In the backdrop of World War II, Princess Elizabeth was not only learning and emerging as a powerful royal figure due to her efforts in the political landscape but also burgeoning her romance with Prince Philip, her future husband.

The couple's initial meeting had happened in 1934 at a family wedding. Elizabeth, then only eight, and Philip, thirteen, shared a distant familial connection, being second cousins once removed through King Christian IX of Denmark and third cousins through Queen Victoria. Their paths crossed again in 1937, but their third meeting sparked the romance. In July 1939, at the Royal Naval College in Dartmouth, thirteen-year-old Elizabeth found herself deeply enamored with the eighteen-year-old Philip. From then on, they began exchanging letters, kindling the flames of a young love.

By the time their engagement was announced on July 9, 1947, Elizabeth was twenty-one. This announcement stirred a mix of reactions. Philip, though a British subject and a Royal Navy officer, faced scrutiny for his Greek and Danish origins and his financially humble background. His sisters' marriages to German noblemen with Nazi connections added to the controversy. Despite these challenges, including initial reservations from Elizabeth's mother, their love persevered.

Prior to their marriage, Philip made significant changes. He renounced his Greek and Danish royal titles, converted from Greek Orthodoxy to Anglicanism, and adopted the surname Mountbatten from his mother's British family. He was also made Duke of Edinburgh and granted the title His Royal Highness just before their wedding.

Their wedding, held on November 20, 1947, at Westminster Abbey, was a momentous event. It brought a sense of joy and celebration to a post-war Britain still in recovery. The couple's wedding was a grand affair, with Elizabeth's dress designed by Sir Norman Hartnell, inspired by a Botticelli painting. Elizabeth's iconic wedding dress symbolized both austerity and elegance, as she used ration coupons to purchase the fabric. Their nine-foot tall wedding cake featured their coats of arms and sugar figures of their favorite activities. Despite the nation's economic difficulties, the couple received over 2,500 gifts from around the world.

After their wedding, they spent their honeymoon at Philip's uncle's estate in Hampshire and later at the Scottish Balmoral estate. In the early years of their marriage, especially during their time in Malta, the couple enjoyed a simpler, more carefree life away from the royal spotlight. The newlyweds initially settled at Windlesham Moor, near Windsor Castle, before moving to Clarence House in London. From 1949 to 1951, the couple spent significant time in Malta, where Philip was stationed with the Royal Navy. Elizabeth and Philip's life in Malta offered them a semblance of normalcy away from the royal spotlight.

In Malta, Princess Elizabeth, living as the wife of a naval officer, often attended lively parties. These gatherings were known for their spirited atmosphere, where utensils and food playfully flew through the air, as recounted by her lady-in-waiting,[4] Henriette Abel Smith.

In the English monarchy, a lady-in-waiting is a woman who attends to a queen, queen consort, or princess. The role is largely ceremonial and social in modern times, but historically, it involved a mix of personal service and advising. Ladies-in-waiting are selected from among the nobility or those with close ties to the royal family, and their duties can include accompanying the royal lady on official engagements, helping her with correspondence, and various other tasks to assist in her day-to-day life and public duties.

In moments of excessive exuberance, Prince Philip would take measures to ensure safety by having the ladies sit atop the piano, away from any playful mischief.

This period of joyous social life was soon complemented by a significant family development. Their family began to grow with the birth of Prince Charles in 1948 and Princess Anne in 1950. In anticipation of these births, King George VI issued letters patent—official legal documents granted by a monarch or government granting a right or title—allowing their children to be styled as royal princes and princesses. This privilege was especially significant because their father, Philip, had relinquished his royal titles, which would have otherwise left his children without the styling typically afforded to the offspring of British royalty. The letters patent thus ensured that the children would hold titles befitting their status within the royal family.

Through these early years, Elizabeth and Philip navigated the complexities of their public and private lives. Their love story was more than a simple royal romance; it was a journey of mutual respect, adaptation, and profound commitment. It set the stage for Elizabeth's eventual ascension to the throne and the many decades they would spend together as Britain's longest-reigning monarch and her consort.

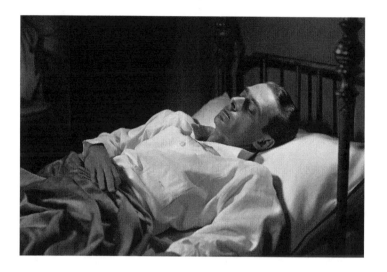

In 1951, only a few years after the wedding of the princess, King George VI's health was visibly failing, marking a pivotal shift in royal responsibilities. Princess Elizabeth, understanding the gravity of her father's condition, began to undertake more royal duties, symbolizing her impending role as the nation's figurehead. Her presence at public events became more frequent, filling in for her ailing father.

This transition was notably evident during her visit to Canada and Washington D.C., in October 1951. It was a trip shadowed by the somber reality that her father's health could take a turn for the worse at any moment. Elizabeth's private secretary, Martin Charteris, carried a draft accession declaration, prepared for the possibility that she might ascend to the throne while abroad.

The year 1952 marked the primary turning point. Elizabeth and her husband, Philip, embarked on a tour destined for Australia and New Zealand, with a stopover in the British colony of Kenya. It was during their stay at Sagana Lodge, after a night at the Treetops Hotel in Kenya, that they received the life-changing news of King George VI's death on February 6th. Prince Philip bore the heavy responsibility of breaking the news to Elizabeth, who, at that moment, had become Queen.

Choosing to retain her name, Elizabeth II ascended the throne. This decision, while respectful of her lineage, stirred discontent in Scotland, as she was the first monarch named Elizabeth to rule there.

Upon her return to the United Kingdom, Queen Elizabeth II and Prince Philip moved into Buckingham Palace. Following the Queen's coronation and the settlement into Buckingham Place, the deep connection between her and Princess Margaret was maintained through a dedicated telephone line between Buckingham Palace and Kensington Palace. It was through this line that the sisters reportedly engaged in daily conversations, sharing laughter and confidences with each other.

The early days of her reign brought forth the question of the royal house's name. Tradition suggested it might take the name of her husband, leading to suggestions like House of Mountbatten or House of Edinburgh. However, Prime Minister Winston Churchill and

Elizabeth's grandmother, Queen Mary, favored retaining the House of Windsor. On April 9th, 1952, Elizabeth declared the royal house would continue as Windsor, a decision that reportedly left Philip feeling marginalized.

The early period of Elizabeth's reign, when she was yet to be crowned, was not just about administrative changes. They were also marked by personal challenges within the royal family. One such challenge was Princess Margaret's wish to marry Peter Townsend, a divorcé with two children. Elizabeth, understanding the complexities of the situation, asked them to wait. The union faced opposition from politicians and the Church of England, which did not permit remarriage after divorce. Ultimately, Margaret chose to forgo the marriage, later marrying Antony Armstrong-Jones in 1960 with whom she had two children.

In the midst of these personal and political upheavals, Queen Elizabeth II prepared for her coronation. Despite the death of Queen Mary on March 24th, 1953, the coronation proceeded as planned on June 2nd, honoring Mary's wish. The ceremony, televised for the first time, was a momentous event, symbolizing a new era in British monarchy. Elizabeth's coronation gown, embroidered with the floral emblems of Commonwealth countries, was a testament to her dedication to her realm and its diverse constituents.

Queen Elizabeth II's early years as monarch were a blend of solemn duty and personal evolution. The death of her father not only marked the end of an era but also ushered in a new age of monarchy under her stewardship. Her journey from a princess stepping in for her father to a queen defining her reign was marked by resilience, adaptability, and a profound sense of duty. These qualities would come to define her decades-long tenure as one of the most respected and enduring monarchs in history.

PART II
A Reign Unseen (1952-1970)

Elizabeth's journey as a monarch had begun long before she ascended the throne. Her accession to the throne in 1952 was not just a personal milestone but also a pivotal moment in the history of the British monarchy. It marked the beginning of her reign over multiple independent states, a role she embraced with dedication.

When the Queen inherited the Crown, the court she was put in was similar to that of her Grandfather, George V. The old guard courtiers were similar, and they were holding onto the traditions that started at the beginning of the century. Their courtiers were often seen as a stuffy bunch who weren't too fond of the press and media. However, the period following the war was marked by significant societal and economic shifts in Britain. From a formidable industrial power, the country transitioned to a service economy, embracing innovation and modernity. This change was mirrored in the monarchy under Elizabeth's reign. The Queen, influenced by her husband Prince Philip, a known modernizer, began the process of adapting the Royal Family to the changing times. This adaptation was not only a matter of changing traditions but also a reflection of the changing face of Britain and its place in the world.

In 1953, a year after her accession, Elizabeth embarked on an ambitious seven-month tour around the world, covering over 40,000 miles by land, sea, and air. This tour was not just a journey through different geographies but also a profound statement of her commitment to the Commonwealth. She visited thirteen countries, marking her presence as a reigning monarch in nations like Australia and New Zealand for the first time. The magnitude of her impact was visible in the massive crowds that gathered to see her, with three-quarters of Australia's population estimated to have caught a glimpse of their Queen.

Starting with her reign, Queen Elizabeth II met with every US President from Harry S. Truman to Joe Biden, except for Lyndon B. Johnson. This particular exclusion wasn't due to any deliberate oversight or diplomatic tension but resulted from the lack of a mutually suitable occasion for an official visit or meeting during Johnson's term (1963-1969). Despite the absence of a direct meeting between Queen Elizabeth II and President Johnson, this circumstance was not due to any intention to avoid diplomatic engagements. Queen Elizabeth's interactions with all other US presidents were significant not merely as formalities but also as pivotal moments that reinforced the "special relationship" between the United Kingdom and the United States. Her state visit in 1957, hosted by President Dwight D. Eisenhower, and her address to the United Nations General Assembly during this visit are prime examples of the profound impact of these engagements.

As a young monarch, her speech to an international body predominantly led by men was a significant moment, demonstrating her global stature and influence. In June 1982, she became the first British monarch to address a joint session of the U.S. Congress, underlining the significance of the transatlantic alliance.

Elizabeth's reign saw her become a symbol of continuity and stability, navigating the complexities of constitutional conventions and political changes with grace and wisdom. Her travels were not just about state visits but about strengthening the bonds within the Commonwealth. She wasn't just the most widely traveled head of state; she was a binding force, a presence that transcended borders and cultures.

The early days of the Queen's reign faced not just political challenges but also economic hardships. After the World Wars, Britain had fallen down in its prestige and financial status and primarily needed money from the United States to rebuild its economy. The Queen's reign saw the implementation of various social and economic reforms aimed at rebuilding the nation's economy and improving living standards. The establishment of the National Health Service in 1948 and the expansion of the welfare state were significant steps in this direction. While the Queen played no direct role in these policies, her reign represented a period of social transformation and progress.

Her annual Christmas broadcasts, a tradition started by her father, became a medium through which she could address her subjects directly, sharing her thoughts and reflections on the year gone by. These broadcasts, devoid of political agendas, were a way for the Queen to connect with her people, offering words of hope, encouragement, and unity.

Becoming a model head for the modernizing world, Queen Elizabeth II's 1957 Christmas broadcast from the Sandringham House ushered in a new era of monarchial communication. Through the "new medium" of television, Britons saw and heard their Queen for the first time, experiencing a message that balanced technological advancement with timeless values like faith, morality, and honesty.

Thus, within the complex landscape of Post-War Britain, the Queen was dealing with all sorts of sociopolitical changes, from a falling economy to a world with rapidly rising technology.

The Commonwealth

In the wake of World War II, Britain faced the monumental task of rebuilding a battered nation and redefining its role on the global stage. Queen Elizabeth II ascended to the throne in 1952, in a Britain still recovering from the devastation of war. Her coronation symbolized not just a new reign but also the hopes and aspirations of a country seeking to rebuild itself. The Queen's role, largely ceremonial, became a beacon of stability and continuity for a populace eager to move past the hardships of war.

One of the most defining aspects of Elizabeth's early reign was the decolonization of the British Empire. The process had begun even before she became Queen, but it gained momentum during her reign.

Countries in Asia, such as India, Pakistan, and Ceylon (now Sri Lanka), achieved independence shortly after the war, setting a precedent for other colonies. Elizabeth's role in this process was mainly symbolic, but she represented a new era of British leadership, one that was more inclined toward a peaceful transition than colonial dominance.

The evolution of the Commonwealth realms, where Queen Elizabeth remained head of state, highlighted a modern form of monarchy. These independent countries, including Canada, Australia, and New Zealand, maintained a constitutional link with the British monarchy while comprehensively governing themselves. This unique arrangement demonstrated the adaptability of the monarchy under Elizabeth II, fostering a sense of shared history and identity across diverse nations.

The Queen also met with numerous colonial leaders, both publicly and privately, providing a platform for dialogue and understanding during the complex process of decolonization. Her interactions with figures like Kwame Nkrumah of Ghana and Jawaharlal Nehru of India helped to foster relationships with newly independent nations.

The 1950s were a turbulent time for the British monarchy, with the Suez Crisis marking a significant challenge. The crisis, which unfolded in 1956, saw Britain, France, and Israel attempt to seize control of the Suez Canal from Egypt. Elizabeth's role during this crisis was that of a silent observer, her personal views and feelings obscured by the veil of monarchy. However, it was rumored that she was opposed to the invasion, a sentiment that added a layer of complexity to her position. The crisis eventually led to the resignation of Prime Minister Sir Anthony Eden, plunging the monarchy into a period of political uncertainty.

Elizabeth's role in appointing Eden's successor highlighted the nuanced balance of power and influence she held. She was advised by a constellation of political figures, from Lord Salisbury to Winston Churchill, eventually appointing Harold Macmillan as the new prime minister. This decision and the process leading to it underscored the intricate dance between the monarchy and the government, a dance that Elizabeth mastered over the years.

The years following the Suez Crisis were not without their challenges. Elizabeth faced criticism, most notably from Lord Altrincham in 1957, who accused her of being out of touch with the people. This criticism was met with public outrage, reflecting the deep connection and reverence the public held for their Queen. Despite these challenges, Elizabeth's resolve never wavered. She continued to carry out her duties with the same dedication and poise, embodying the very essence of the British monarchy.

Her state visits were not just diplomatic gestures but reflections of her commitment to the Commonwealth and its people. In 1957, she addressed the United Nations General Assembly, representing not just the United Kingdom but the entire Commonwealth. Her travels took her to Canada, the United States, and countries across Asia and Africa. In each visit, she left an indelible mark, not just as a monarch but as a symbol of unity and strength.

Throughout her reign, her efforts of enhancing the Commonwealth remained admirable. The Queen's contributions extended to numerous trusts and initiatives across the Commonwealth. The Queen Elizabeth Diamond Jubilee Trust, for instance, made significant strides in combating avoidable causes of blindness, providing millions of treatments and surgeries to eliminate trachoma in several Commonwealth countries. Furthermore, The Queen's Young Leaders programme recognized and supported young individuals making remarkable contributions to their communities across the Commonwealth.

Additionally, the Queen's Commonwealth Canopy, launched in 2015, became a testament to her commitment to environmental conservation, involving over forty-five countries in a network of forest conservation initiatives aimed at preserving vast areas of land in their natural state for future generations.

Queen Elizabeth II's dedication to the Commonwealth was profound, encompassing extensive international diplomacy, the nurturing of cultural ties, and significant charitable efforts. Her reign saw her undertake more than 200 visits to Commonwealth countries, covering almost every nation in the association and often making numerous return trips. Remarkably, a third of all her overseas visits were to Commonwealth countries, underlining her commitment to these nations. Her first official overseas visit as Princess Elizabeth in 1947 included a significant tour of South Africa, Zimbabwe, and Botswana, where she delivered a broadcast on her twenty-first birthday, expressing her vision and hope for the Commonwealth's future.

Queen Elizabeth II's engagements with the Commonwealth extended far beyond ceremonial duties, marking her reign with a deep and impactful commitment to its cultural and developmental initiatives. Her attendance at twenty-two Commonwealth Heads of Government Meetings and seven Commonwealth Games underscores this dedication, highlighting her role in fostering unity, cooperation, and a sense of shared purpose among the diverse nations of the Commonwealth.

The Commonwealth Games, a cornerstone of this engagement, stand out as one of the world's foremost sports competitions. Initiated in 1930 in Hamilton, Canada, and held every four years, these games have become a celebration of athletic achievement and cultural exchange among the Commonwealth nations. Despite interruptions in 1942 and 1946 due to World War II, the Games have continually showcased sports popular across the member countries, such as athletics, swimming, lawn bowls, and rugby sevens. Reflecting the evolving interests and cultures of its participants, the range of sports has expanded over the years, embodying the Commonwealth's diversity and the Queen's commitment to celebrating it.

Moreover, Queen Elizabeth's interactions with Commonwealth leaders during her reign were instrumental in strengthening the bonds within this international community. Hosting numerous heads of state, she facilitated dialogue and understanding, which were pivotal in shaping the Commonwealth's future direction. These engagements were more than formalities; they were vital opportunities to foster a sense of community and mutual support, reinforcing the Commonwealth's values of equality, respect, and understanding.

Through her dedication to both the Commonwealth Games and the Heads of Government Meetings, Queen Elizabeth II demonstrated a profound commitment to the Commonwealth's ideals.

Family Matters

Queen Elizabeth II's family began increasing with the birth of her first child, Prince Charles, on November 14, 1948. His arrival marked a joyous occasion in post-war Britain, bringing hope and a sense of continuity to the monarchy. Born at Buckingham Palace, Charles was the first child of Princess Elizabeth and Philip.

In the early years of his life, Prince Charles experienced a childhood that was simultaneously extraordinary and yet, in some ways, typical for a child of his status. The young prince was mostly raised by nannies, as was customary for royal children. His early education took place at home under the guidance of governesses. This isolation from the outside world was partly due to his royal status and partly a reflection of the times.

As he grew older, Charles's education followed a path befitting a future king. He attended Hill House School in West London, followed by Cheam Preparatory School and then the prestigious Gordonstoun School in Scotland, reflecting his father's educational choices. These experiences, while giving him an excellent academic grounding, also exposed him to the challenges of being outside the royal bubble for the first time.

Throughout his upbringing, Prince Charles was constantly aware of his destiny as the future King of England. His mother's ascension to the throne in 1952, when he was just three years old, placed him directly in the line of succession. This knowledge and the expectations that came with it would shape much of his early life and his relationship with his family and the public.

After Prince Charles, Queen Elizabeth II had three more children: Princess Anne, born on August 15, 1950; Prince Andrew, born on February 19, 1960; and Prince Edward, born on March 10, 1964. Each child brought a unique dynamic to the royal family, and the Queen's relationship with each was distinct.

Princess Anne, the Queen's only daughter, shared a close bond with her mother, united by their mutual love of horses and equestrian sports. Anne's strong-willed and independent nature seemed to resonate with the Queen, who had always admired strength of character.

Prince Andrew, born a decade after Anne, entered a royal family that was already well-established in the public eye. The Queen's relationship with Andrew was described as affectionate, with Andrew often considered to have been her favorite son, a claim that was a topic of public speculation.

The youngest, Prince Edward, was born at a time when the Queen had more experience balancing her royal duties with family life. Edward's upbringing was said to be more relaxed, and he shared a warm and close relationship with both of his parents.

Behind the grandeur and formality of her public persona, Queen Elizabeth II's life within the walls of Buckingham Palace and other royal residences was marked by a deep commitment to her family. Despite the demands of her role, she endeavored to be present in the lives of her children–Charles, Anne, Andrew, and Edward. But, Elizabeth's early years with her children were also marked by long periods of separation due to her duties, including a six-month tour of the Commonwealth in 1953. This separation meant that the children often spent more time with nannies and in the care of the nursery staff. However, the family valued their time together, cherishing moments like Christmas at Sandringham and summers at Balmoral, when they could enjoy each other's company away from public duties.

The Queen's relationship with Prince Charles was of particular interest over the years. As the heir apparent, Charles received much attention and guidance from his mother. However, the nature of her role as monarch and his as the future king often meant that their relationship was as much institutional as it was familial. This dynamic, while necessary, sometimes led to a perceived distance between mother and son, especially in the public eye.

Elizabeth II's role as a mother extended far beyond the nurturing of her children; she also took on the intricate management of the royal household, balancing the demands of both duties with grace and precision. In her efforts to provide stability and normalcy for her family amidst the grandeur of palace life, she implemented various traditions and routines, fostering an environment where her children could thrive despite the pressures of their royal status. Through her dedication to familial harmony and her meticulous attention to detail, she set a strong example of maternal leadership within the monarchy.

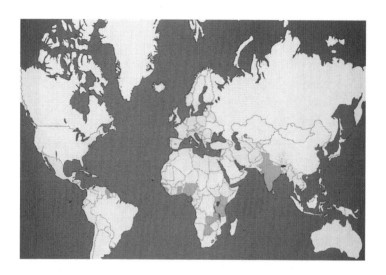

The 1960s in Britain were a time of remarkable social and cultural upheaval, a period that reshaped the nation's identity and its view of the monarchy. Queen Elizabeth, a symbol of continuity amidst these rapid changes, played a nuanced role during this transformative decade. This era, often characterized by vibrant social movements and the decolonization of the British Empire, demanded a delicate balance from the monarchy, particularly from the Queen, who was navigating both her country's evolving landscape and her own evolving role as a monarch.

A significant aspect of the 1960s was the acceleration of the decolonization of Africa and the Caribbean. This period saw more than twenty countries gaining independence from Britain, marking a substantial transition towards self-government. This wave of change not only altered Britain's global standing but also impacted its national identity.

One of the most notable events in this process was the unilateral declaration of independence by Rhodesian Prime Minister Ian Smith in 1965.[5] Smith declared loyalty to Queen Elizabeth, naming her "Queen of Rhodesia" despite her formal dismissal of him. This act was in opposition to the movement towards majority rule and resulted in international sanctions against Rhodesia. For the Queen, this presented a complex situation where she had to balance her ceremonial role as a constitutional monarch with the changing political realities of the Commonwealth.

In 1966, a significant challenge to the Queen's public image occurred following the Aberfan disaster in Wales. A mining spoil tip collapsed, engulfing a school and houses in the village, leading to the tragic loss of 144 lives, including 116 children. The Queen's decision to delay her visit to the disaster site for eight days, based on advice she received, was met with criticism. This incident underscored the evolving expectations of the public from the monarchy in times of national tragedy. It was a learning moment for the Queen, who later expressed regret for the delay, highlighting a shift in her understanding of the monarchy's role in providing moral and emotional support to the nation.

Rhodesia's Unilateral Declaration of Independence (UDI) was a statement adopted by the Cabinet of Rhodesia on 11 November 1965, announcing that Southern Rhodesia or simply Rhodesia, a British territory in southern Africa that had governed itself since 1923, now regarded itself as an independent sovereign state.

The 1960s were not just about political transformations, they were also a time of significant social and cultural shifts. The emergence of youth culture, the women's liberation movement, and the expansion of the mass media reshaped British society. In this context, the monarchy, led by Queen Elizabeth II, had to find its place in a society that was rapidly modernizing and becoming more informal.

In an attempt to adapt to the changing times and offer a glimpse into the life of the royal family, a documentary titled "Royal Family" was released in 1969. This was a groundbreaking moment, as it was one of the first times the public got an intimate look at the life of the royals. The documentary was immensely popular, drawing in over thirty million viewers in England alone. It was a bold move aimed at humanizing the royal family and making them more relatable to the public.

The same year also saw significant achievements in space exploration, with Queen Elizabeth II involved in the historic Apollo Eleven moon landing. She sent a message of goodwill which was carried to the moon by the astronauts, and later, she met with the astronauts at Buckingham Palace, marking a significant moment in her reign and reflecting the global reach and influence of her monarchy.

Queen Elizabeth's approach to these changes was characterized by a gradual adaptation. While maintaining the dignity and traditions of the monarchy, she also made subtle changes in royal engagements and public appearances, reflecting a more modern and relatable image. This approach helped the monarchy remain relevant and respected in a society that was increasingly questioning traditional institutions.

The 1960s were a decade of significant change for Britain. As the nation navigated through the challenges of decolonization, social transformations, and national tragedies, Queen Elizabeth's responses and adaptations were critical in maintaining the monarchy's relevance. Her ability to balance tradition with the necessity for change, her responses to national crises, and her navigation through the evolving landscape of modern Britain were crucial in shaping the monarchy as an enduring institution in a rapidly changing world.

We're Halfway There: A Note from Scott Matthews

Dear Esteemed Reader,

Thank you for joining me on this historical journey within the pages of *A Brief History of Queen Elizabeth II.*

As an author, I am passionate about connecting with readers like you. Your perspective and opinion is super important to me! That's why I want to invite you to leave a review on Amazon.

Your review is more than just a critique, your review allows me, Scott Matthews, to understand what resonated with you and how I can continue to provide engaging and informative content.

If you don't know how to leave a review, don't worry, I'll help you out. First, visit the Amazon page and look for the book in your orders, and select it. Once there, scroll down to the "Customer Reviews" section and click on the "Write a customer review" button. Otherwise scan the QR code (or click it if you're on a Kindle) to share your thoughts.

Feel free to express your thoughts. Your support and thoughtful critique are immensely appreciated. Thank you for reading!

PART III
A Steadfast Crown (1971-2002)

The Troubles and Beyond

The latter half of the twentieth century, particularly the 1970s, presented a complex set of challenges for Queen Elizabeth II and the British monarchy. This era was significantly marked by the Northern Ireland conflict, known as "The Troubles" alongside the overarching backdrop of the Cold War and shifting global politics. Queen Elizabeth II navigated her role in a world fraught with intricate international relations and intense domestic issues.

The Northern Ireland conflict was a complex and multifaceted conflict that began in the late 1960s and lasted until the Good Friday Agreement in 1998. It primarily stemmed from deep-seated political, religious, and nationalistic divisions. The conflict was rooted in the partition of Ireland in 1921, which led to the creation of Northern Ireland as a part of the United Kingdom, predominantly Protestant, and the Republic of Ireland, predominantly Catholic.

"The Troubles" escalated from civil rights marches and protests against discrimination of the Catholic/Nationalist minority in Northern Ireland into a violent and protracted conflict. It involved paramilitary groups like the Irish Republican Army (IRA), which sought unification with the Republic of Ireland, and loyalist paramilitaries, which fought to keep Northern Ireland within the UK.

Throughout the 1970s, the conflict intensified, with tragic events such as Bloody Sunday in 1972, where British soldiers shot twenty-six unarmed civilians. As a constitutional monarch, Queen Elizabeth II's role was primarily symbolic. However, her actions and responses were crucial in conveying a stance of neutrality and a commitment to peace and reconciliation. Her visits to Northern Ireland and meetings with leaders from both communities were seen as significant gestures towards fostering dialogue and understanding.

The journey to peace in Northern Ireland was long and arduous. The efforts towards reconciliation involved various British and Irish governments and international mediation. The turning point came with the signing of the Good Friday Agreement in 1998, which was a major political development in the peace process. This agreement established a new, devolved government in Northern Ireland and laid the groundwork for future cooperation and peace.

Queen Elizabeth II's role in the peace process, though indirect, was symbolically significant. In 2012, in a historic gesture of reconciliation, she met with Martin McGuinness, a former IRA commander and then deputy First Minister of Northern Ireland, and shook hands with him. This event was emblematic of the strides taken towards peace and the Queen's support for the ongoing reconciliation process.

During the Cold War era, Queen Elizabeth II's role in international relations was underscored by her engagements in diplomatic and state affairs. Her state visits, including those to countries within the Eastern bloc, were pivotal in maintaining and promoting Britain's diplomatic relationships amidst global tensions.

The Queen's diplomatic efforts were not limited to Europe. Her constitutional role required her to navigate a range of international issues, from the decolonization process in Africa and the Caribbean to engaging with new global players on the international stage.

In the realm of domestic politics, the 1970s also presented significant challenges. The Queen's constitutional role was highlighted during moments such as the 1974 general election, which resulted in a hung parliament. Her decisions during this period, including the appointment of Harold Wilson as Prime Minister, underscored her role in the UK's parliamentary democracy.

The 1970s, with the backdrop of "The Troubles" in Northern Ireland and the Cold War, were a period of significant challenge and change for Queen Elizabeth II and the British monarchy. The Queen's responses to these challenges, marked by a commitment to her role and a sensitivity to the complexities of the era, helped to maintain the monarchy's stability and relevance during one of the most turbulent periods in recent history. Her actions, though often symbolic, played a crucial part in supporting the path to peace in Northern Ireland and upholding the dignity and neutrality of the monarchy in a rapidly changing world.

Silver Jubilee and Personal Loss

In 1977, the United Kingdom and the Commonwealth celebrated Queen Elizabeth II's Silver Jubilee, marking twenty-five years since her accession to the throne. This milestone was more than a mere celebration; it was a reaffirmation of the Queen's enduring presence and the stability she brought to the monarchy in a period of rapid change.

The Silver Jubilee was a nationwide celebration characterized by street parties, parades, and special events across the Commonwealth. In every corner of the UK, communities came together, reflecting the sense of unity and national pride that the Queen had come to embody. This jubilee was not just a celebration of the Queen's twenty-five years on the throne but also a testament to her ability to adapt and modernize the monarchy while maintaining its traditions.

One of the most significant events was the Queen's jubilee tour, which took her to various parts of the UK and the Commonwealth. These visits were not merely ceremonial; they were a way for the Queen to connect with her subjects from all walks of life. The enthusiasm and warmth with which she was received during these tours were indicative of the deep affection and respect she had garnered over the years.

The Silver Jubilee also served as a reflection of how the monarchy had evolved under the Queen's reign. Since her accession in 1952, Queen Elizabeth II had witnessed and navigated through significant political, social, and technological changes. Her steadfastness and dedication to her duties during these changes helped solidify her reign, making the Silver Jubilee not just a celebration of the past but also a hopeful look towards the future.

Amidst the public celebrations and duties, the Queen faced profound personal challenges, particularly in the early twenty-first century. The deaths of her sister, Princess Margaret, and her mother, the Queen Mother, within weeks of each other in 2002, were a significant personal loss for her.

Princess Margaret, the Queen's younger sister, passed away on February 9, 2002, after suffering a stroke. Margaret had been a vibrant and vital part of the Queen's life, sharing the burdens and joys of royal life. Her passing left a void in the Queen's personal life, taking away not just a sister but a lifelong confidante. Despite their differing personalities and the divergent paths their lives had taken, the bond between the sisters endured as an unbreakable connection, profound in its depth and like a primal force that shaped their very beings.

The death of the Queen Mother on March 30, 2002, at the age of 101, was another profound loss for Queen Elizabeth II. The Queen Mother had been a pillar of strength and support, not just for the Queen but for the entire nation, particularly during the difficult years of World War II. Her longevity and resilience had made her a beloved national figure, and her passing marked the end of an era.

These back-to-back personal losses came at a time when the monarchy was facing public scrutiny and challenges. The Queen's handling of these tragedies was a testament to her stoic and resilient nature. She balanced her private grief with her public duties, demonstrating her commitment to her role even in the face of personal sorrow.

The way Queen Elizabeth II dealt with her personal losses while continuing to fulfill her public duties was remarkable. Her ability to maintain her composure and carry on with her responsibilities during these difficult times was a reflection of her strength of character and her deep sense of duty. It was also during this time that the public saw a more personal side of the Queen, one that was not often visible behind the formalities of her role.

Her resilience in the face of personal tragedy also served to deepen the public's affection and respect for her. The nation sympathized with the Queen's losses, seeing in her not just a monarch but a person who, like anyone else, experienced the pain of losing loved ones.

The period encompassing the Silver Jubilee and the subsequent personal losses of Princess Margaret and the Queen Mother was a time of both celebration and sorrow for Queen Elizabeth II. The jubilee marked a significant milestone in her reign, showcasing her success in leading the monarchy through decades of change. At the same time, the personal tragedies she faced brought to light her human side, revealing the strength and resilience that had characterized her reign.

Changing Tides and Modernization

The latter half of the twentieth century was characterized by a series of events that tested the resilience and adaptability of the monarchy, leading to significant changes in its relationship with the public and the way it engaged with modernization and technological advancements.

The process of devolution, which saw the establishment of the Scottish Parliament and National Assembly for Wales, was a pivotal moment in the country's history. Queen Elizabeth II played a crucial role in this transition, formally opening these new legislatures. Her involvement symbolized the monarchy's support for the changing political landscape of the UK.

At the same time, the rise of the Internet and media revolutionized the way information was disseminated and consumed. The Queen, recognizing the importance of staying connected with her subjects in an increasingly digital world, embraced these technological advancements. This period saw the royal family becoming more accessible and transparent, with the Queen herself making significant strides in engaging with the public through various media platforms.

In 1979, Queen Elizabeth II also embarked on a historic tour of the Middle East, becoming the first British monarch to visit the Gulf States. Her visit included stops in Kuwait, Bahrain, Saudi Arabia, Qatar, the United Arab Emirates, and Oman. This tour was significant as it came at a time of increasing economic and political importance of the Gulf region in global affairs, particularly due to oil. Her meetings with leaders like Sheikh Jaber of Kuwait and Sheikh Isa of Bahrain were pivotal in strengthening diplomatic relations and trade ties with these emerging powers.

The Queen's meeting with Pope John Paul II in 1980 was a momentous occasion, symbolizing the strengthening of relations between the Anglican Church and the Catholic Church. This meeting, held at the Vatican, was significant in promoting interfaith dialogue and mutual respect between different religious traditions.

During the Trooping the Colour ceremony in 1981, a shocking incident occurred as Elizabeth rode down The Mall in London. A young assailant fired six shots at her, later found to be blanks. Despite this alarming event, the Queen's composure was remarkable, showcasing her resilience and ability to maintain calm in the face of danger.

The Queen's sense of duty and personal strength were further evident in 1982. Her son Prince Andrew's service in the Falklands War was a source of both pride and anxiety for her. Amidst the backdrop of Prince Andrew's service in the Falklands War, Queen Elizabeth II's sense of duty and resilience was profoundly tested by a major security breach at Buckingham Palace. This year, which brought both pride and concern for the royal family, also witnessed a defiant intrusion into the very heart of the British monarchy.

Buckingham Palace, a symbol of British heritage and the residence of the royal family, accustomed to hosting thousands annually for various state functions, found itself the target of an unwelcome visitor. On July 9, 1982, Michael Fagan, a 31-year-old Londoner with a background as a painter and decorator, shockingly scaled the palace's perimeter wall, ascended a drainpipe, and entered through an unlocked window after a night of drinking. His actions not only breached the palace's security but also led him directly into the private quarters of Queen Elizabeth II, marking one of the most significant security lapses in the palace's history.

Fagan's intrusion into the Queen's bedroom, where he engaged in conversation with Her Majesty, was a moment of unexpected danger met with remarkable poise by the Queen. Despite pressing an alarm button and calling for help, there was a delay in the security response, showcasing a breakdown in the palace's security protocols. It was only through the Queen's calm demeanor and quick thinking, eventually getting through to a maid, that led to Fagan's detention. This incident was not Fagan's first unauthorized palace entry, revealing a shocking vulnerability in the royal residence's security measures. Fagan had previously entered Buckingham Palace, navigating its corridors and even sitting on the throne, undetected until his presence in the Queen's bedroom set off alarms. This breach sparked a public scandal, leading to a resignation offer from the UK Home Secretary William Whitelaw, which the Queen declined. Legally, Fagan faced no charges for trespassing due to the incident's unique nature involving royal premises. However, he was tried for theft related to another intrusion where he consumed Prince Charles's wine. Post-arrest, Fagan underwent psychiatric evaluation and was temporarily committed to a mental health institution. This extraordinary breach highlighted the multifaceted challenges faced by Queen Elizabeth II during her reign, from managing personal anxieties over her son's wartime service to navigating diplomatic relations and addressing significant security oversights within her own residence.

The 1980s were a tumultuous time for the royal family, marked by intense media scrutiny. Sensational stories in the press, often speculative or unverified, became common. Queen Elizabeth II's relationship with Margaret Thatcher, the Prime Minister of the United Kingdom from 1979 to 1990, was one of the most scrutinized and speculated aspects of her reign. This period was marked by significant social and economic changes in Britain, and the dynamic between the monarch and the Prime Minister inevitably became a topic of public interest.

The Queen and Margaret Thatcher, although contemporaries in age, had markedly different personalities and backgrounds. Elizabeth, born into the royal family and ascending the throne at a young age, had a deep sense of duty and tradition. Thatcher, on the other hand, came from a modest background and rose through the ranks of the Conservative Party, becoming the first female Prime Minister of the UK. Their differing perspectives were reflected in their approaches to governance and public policy.

The Queen and the Prime Minister had weekly private meetings, a traditional engagement between the monarch and the head of government. These meetings were confidential, and both parties maintained a professional relationship. However, the media often speculated about potential disagreements, particularly regarding Thatcher's economic policies and social reforms, which were seen as contributing to social division and unrest in the 1980s. Reports occasionally surfaced suggesting that the Queen was concerned about the impact of these policies on the nation, especially in terms of unemployment, social unrest, and Thatcher's stance on apartheid South Africa. However, these reports were often based on speculation and unverified sources. The palace rarely commented on political matters, adhering to the constitutional principle that the monarch remains politically neutral.

Despite any personal or ideological differences, both the Queen and Thatcher had a mutual respect for their respective constitutional roles. Thatcher, as the elected head of government, was responsible for policy and governance, while the Queen's role was largely ceremonial and symbolic, serving as a unifying figure for the nation. It's widely acknowledged that both adhered to these boundaries, understanding the importance of maintaining the stability and continuity of the constitutional monarchy. After Thatcher left office, the Queen bestowed upon her two of the highest honors in her personal gift: membership in the Order of Merit and the Order of the Garter.[6]

---

[6] The Order of Merit and the Order of the Garter are two of the highest honors that can be bestowed in the United Kingdom, both of which are in the personal gift of the monarch, meaning they are awarded without the need for governmental advice. The Order of Merit (OM) was established in 1902 by King Edward VII; it recognizes distinguished service in the armed forces, science, literature, art, and the promotion of culture. The Order of the Garter (KG) was founded by King Edward III in 1348; it is the oldest and most senior order of knighthood in the British honors system.

This gesture was seen as a sign of the Queen's respect for Thatcher's service to the country, regardless of any personal or political differences that might have existed.

In a similar vein, Elizabeth's state visit to China in 1986 was a historic milestone, marking her as the first British monarch to visit the country. This visit, which included moments of cultural exchange and humor, also played a role in discussions about the future of Hong Kong. This visit was crucial for strengthening diplomatic ties and discussing the future of Hong Kong, ahead of its 1997 handover. The Queen's engagement with Chinese leaders and her visit to key cultural sites underscored the importance of fostering mutual understanding and respect between the two nations.

Keeping in tune with her altruistic nature, in 1987, Queen Elizabeth II opened the first dedicated AIDS ward at London's Middlesex Hospital. Notably, she made headlines by shaking hands, without gloves, with HIV/AIDS patients. This act was seen as a powerful statement against the stigma associated with the disease at the time. Her gesture was a significant moment in public health awareness and showed her willingness to engage with and understand contemporary social issues.

But, the late 1980s and early 1990s were also periods of both personal and institutional challenges for Queen Elizabeth II. The public participation of young royals in a charity game show was met with ridicule, and her role in the politically charged environment of countries like Fiji demonstrated the global reach of her influence. The early 1990s brought more personal trials, culminating in her description of 1992 as an "annus horribilis," a year marked by family strife and public controversy.

A key event of 1992 was when on November 20, 1992, a devastating fire broke out at Windsor Castle, one of the residences of Queen Elizabeth II. Originating from Queen Victoria's Private Chapel due to a faulty spotlight, the fire rapidly engulfed the area, ultimately destroying 115 rooms, including nine State Rooms. St. George's Hall, adjacent to the chapel, was severely affected. Despite the fire's intensity, a successful evacuation of priceless works of art from the Royal Collection was conducted, with only two items being lost. The fire, which took fifteen hours to extinguish, prompted a significant restoration project led by the Duke of Edinburgh. This restoration embraced both a return to historical accuracy and modern reinterpretation. For instance, the new Lantern Lobby replaced the space of the original chapel, and St. George's Hall was reconstructed to reflect its fourteenth century origins, yet with a contemporary perspective. Remarkably, the restoration was completed exactly five years later, on November 20, 1997, coinciding with Queen Elizabeth II and Prince Philip's golden wedding anniversary. This event not only marked a significant moment in the history of Windsor Castle but also exemplified the resilience and dedication to heritage under Queen Elizabeth II's reign.

The untimely and tragic death of Princess Diana in August 1997 was not only a profound personal loss for the royal family but also a moment of unprecedented crisis for the monarchy under Queen Elizabeth II's reign. Diana's death marked a pivotal moment, bringing to the fore the delicate relationship between the royal family and public sentiment.

Initially, the Queen's response to Diana's death was in keeping with royal tradition and protocol, which emphasized privacy and restraint in matters of personal grief. The royal family remained at Balmoral, their private residence in Scotland, to provide support and comfort to Princes William and Harry, Diana's sons. This decision, while made with the well-being of her grandsons in mind, was met with public discontent. The absence of an immediate public statement from the Queen and the lack of a flag flown at half-mast over Buckingham Palace were perceived as a lack of empathy and respect for the beloved Princess Diana.

The public's reaction was intense and emotional, with an outpouring of grief that was both unprecedented and unexpected. The sea of flowers outside Kensington Palace and the spontaneous public memorials highlighted the depth of affection and admiration that the public felt for Diana. The Queen, understanding the unique circumstances and the public's need for a more visible expression of grief from the monarchy, made a significant departure from tradition.

In a response that demonstrated both her adaptability and sensitivity to the mood of the nation, Queen Elizabeth II returned to London earlier than planned. She made a rare live television broadcast to the nation, paying tribute to Diana's memory. In this broadcast, the Queen expressed her admiration for Diana and her deep concern as a grandmother for Princes William and Harry. This personal and heartfelt address was a meaningful moment, marking a shift in the royal approach to public engagement and communication.

Moreover, the Queen's decision to allow for a public funeral with full royal honors, despite Diana no longer being a member of the royal family, was a further acknowledgment of Diana's unique place in the hearts of the people and the history of the monarchy. The funeral, watched by millions around the world, was not just a moment of mourning but also a reflection of the changing dynamics between the monarchy and the public.

However, despite these challenges, Elizabeth II continued to adapt and evolve. In 1992, Queen Elizabeth II made a historic address to the European Parliament in Strasbourg. She was the first British monarch to do so. This event was notable as it occurred during a period of significant change in Europe, post the fall of the Berlin Wall and amidst discussions about the future of the European Union. Her speech, emphasizing the need for unity and the importance of a peaceful and prosperous Europe, was a noteworthy gesture towards Britain's role in the evolving European political landscape.

Her participation in significant events, such as addressing the United States Congress and marking her Ruby Jubilee, showcased her enduring commitment to the role. Her response to the changing times, including the modernization of the monarchy's financial arrangements and her involvement in the devolution process within the UK, demonstrated a willingness to embrace change and modernity.

PART IV
Golden Oldie and Beyond
(2002-2022)

The early years of the twenty-first century were marked by significant milestones and historic moments in Queen Elizabeth II's reign, showcasing her enduring presence as a symbol of continuity and resilience in an ever-changing world.

The year 2002 marked the Golden Jubilee of Queen Elizabeth II, celebrating fifty years of her accession to the throne. This milestone was an occasion of national pride and joy, despite being shadowed by personal losses for the Queen, with the deaths of her sister, Princess Margaret, and her mother. The Golden Jubilee was not just a celebration of the Queen's long service but also a reflection of the nation's journey during those decades.

The Queen embarked on an extensive tour, reaffirming her connection with her subjects across the realms. The tour began memorably in Jamaica, where a power outage at a formal banquet could not dim the spirit of the occasion. Throughout the year, in towns and cities, street parties and commemorative events reflected the enthusiasm and respect for the Queen. The public's response was overwhelming, with a million people participating in the Jubilee celebration in London, reflecting a deep-seated respect and affection for the Queen.

In 2011, Queen Elizabeth II hosted the London Conference on Cyberspace at Buckingham Palace. This event brought together government representatives, industry leaders, and cyber experts from over sixty countries to discuss the future of cyberspace, cybersecurity, and the importance of international cooperation in addressing cyber challenges. The Queen's involvement highlighted her recognition of the growing importance of digital infrastructure and cyber issues on the global stage.

Fast forward to 2012, the Diamond Jubilee commemorated sixty years of Queen Elizabeth's reign. This remarkable event was celebrated across the United Kingdom and the Commonwealth, with various members of the royal family representing the Queen in different regions. The Jubilee was marked by a series of events, including the lighting of beacons worldwide, symbolizing the Queen's enduring influence and the global reach of the monarchy.

Among the most significant events during this period was the Queen's historic state visit to Ireland in May 2011. This visit, the first by a British monarch to the

Republic of Ireland since its independence, was a turning point in Anglo-Irish relations. The visit was an important step in healing historical wounds and building a new relationship based on mutual respect and understanding. It was a testament to the Queen's role in fostering diplomatic relationships and her commitment to reconciliation and peace.

The turn of the millennium saw Queen Elizabeth II embracing the new era with a symbolic gesture as she opened the Millennium Dome in London, a colossal structure designed to celebrate the dawning of the new century and showcase the achievements and aspirations of the modern world.

Her adaptability to changing times was also reflected in her response to global events. Following the 9/11 attacks in the United States, in a significant break from tradition, the Queen ordered the American national anthem to be played during the changing of the guard at Buckingham Palace, a poignant gesture of solidarity.

The incident involving the Daily Mirror also represented a significant challenge in Queen Elizabeth II's reign, highlighting the tension between media freedom and the privacy of the royal family. In 2003, the newspaper became embroiled in a scandal involving a breach of royal confidence, an episode that led to a rare legal intervention by the Queen.

The Daily Mirror had published information obtained in a deceptive manner, which involved a reporter from the newspaper gaining employment as a footman at Buckingham Palace. This undercover operation breached the privacy and security protocols of the royal household. The information gathered and subsequently published provided an unauthorized glimpse into the private lives of the royal family, including personal habits and behind-the-scenes activities at the palace.

This act by the Daily Mirror was not just a breach of journalistic ethics but also a violation of the trust placed in palace staff. The revelation that a reporter could infiltrate the royal household raised serious concerns about security and privacy.

In response to this breach, Queen Elizabeth took the uncommon step of initiating legal action. The royal family, typically refraining from direct engagement in legal disputes, particularly with the press, chose to confront this violation to protect their privacy and uphold the dignity of the monarchy. The legal action taken by the Queen resulted in the Daily Mirror being issued an injunction, preventing further publication of confidential information. Additionally, the newspaper was required to contribute towards the Queen's legal costs.

This legal response was a clear statement from the Queen about the boundaries of acceptable reporting and the respect for the private lives of public figures, even those as public as the royal family. It was a firm stance against the invasive tactics sometimes employed by the press in pursuit of sensational stories.

Throughout this challenge, Queen Elizabeth II's response was measured and dignified. Despite the intrusion into her family's private life, she maintained her composure and continued to fulfill her royal duties with the same commitment and grace that had characterized her reign. This incident did not deter her from her public responsibilities, nor did it diminish her dedication to serving the nation and the Commonwealth.

The Queen's handling of the Daily Mirror incident demonstrated not only her commitment to protecting the privacy and dignity of the royal family but also her resilience in the face of adversity. This episode is indicative of the broader challenges faced by the monarchy in the modern era, balancing public accountability with the right to privacy in an increasingly intrusive media landscape.

In 2007, Queen Elizabeth II celebrated another personal milestone, her diamond wedding anniversary with Prince Philip, marking a partnership that was both a personal support system and a symbol of enduring commitment.

Her speech in 2010 at the UN General Assembly, where she was introduced as "an anchor for our age," reaffirmed her status as a respected global figure. This was followed by a poignant visit to New York, where she opened a memorial garden for British victims of the 9/11 attacks, further solidifying her role in international diplomacy and shared global history. The Queen laid a wreath at the site of the tragedy and met with first responders and families of the victims, showcasing her compassion and support in the face of global tragedy.

Queen Elizabeth's involvement in the Olympics also marked significant milestones. Having opened the 1976 Summer Olympics in Montreal, she repeated this honor at the 2012 Summer Olympics in London, becoming the first head of state to open two Olympic Games in different countries. Her appearance in a short film for the opening ceremony of the London

Olympics, alongside actor Daniel Craig as James Bond, was an unexpected and delightful moment, showcasing her sense of humor and willingness to engage with popular culture.

In 2015, Queen Elizabeth II reached another historic milestone, becoming the longest-reigning British monarch (surpassing the previous record held by her great-great-grandmother, Queen Victoria, who had reigned for sixty-three years and 216 days, from June 20, 1837, until her death on January 22, 1901). This milestone underscored her enduring presence in a role historically dominated by men. This was a moment of reflection rather than celebration for the Queen, who humbly remarked that it was not a record she had ever aspired to. It was a poignant reminder of her lifelong commitment to her role and the changing times she had navigated.

The Golden and Diamond Jubilees, along with the historic state visit to Ireland and other momentous events, encapsulate the essence of Queen Elizabeth II's reign in the early twenty-first century.

The reign of Queen Elizabeth II in the twenty-first century witnessed not only the evolution of the British monarchy but also significant transitions within the royal family itself.

The wedding of Prince William and Kate Middleton on April 29, 2011, was a moment of joy and celebration, marking a significant chapter in the modern narrative of the British monarchy. The union was not just a royal event but a global spectacle, drawing millions of viewers worldwide. It represented a bridge between tradition and modernity, as Kate, a commoner with no aristocratic background, was warmly welcomed into the royal family. This event played a pivotal role in reshaping public perception of the monarchy, making it more relatable and accessible to a new generation. The couple's modern approach to their public roles and their ability to connect with people across different walks of life have been seen as a refreshing change, symbolizing a more inclusive and contemporary monarchy.

The Queen's reign, while largely characterized by stability and continuity, has also encountered significant controversies, particularly involving her son Prince Andrew and grandson Prince Harry. These controversies have not only impacted the royal family's public image but also raised questions about the monarchy's role in contemporary society.

Prince Andrew, the Queen's second son, has been involved in a series of contentious situations, most notably his association with convicted sex offender Jeffrey Epstein. This association brought intense media scrutiny and public criticism, particularly after a widely criticized interview with the BBC in 2019 where Prince Andrew attempted to clarify his relationship with Epstein. His explanations, perceived as unconvincing and insensitive, further damaged his reputation.

The situation escalated when Virginia Giuffre, one of Epstein's accusers, filed a lawsuit against Prince Andrew, alleging that she had been trafficked to him and sexually abused. This legal challenge intensified the controversy, leading to calls for Prince Andrew to step back from public duties.

The Queen's response to her son's situation was a delicate balancing act between her role as a monarch and a mother. While she did not publicly comment on the allegations, the decision for Prince Andrew to step back from public duties was seen as a move to protect the monarchy's image. This step underscored the Queen's commitment to the institution of the monarchy, prioritizing its stability and public standing over individual members' personal controversies.

Prince Harry's decision to step back from royal life, along with his wife, Meghan Markle, was another significant event that posed a challenge to the monarchy. The couple's decision, announced in January 2020, was followed by a candid interview with Oprah Winfrey in 2021, where they discussed their experiences within the royal family, including issues related to mental health and media intrusion.

The interview sparked global conversations about the monarchy, including allegations of racism and lack of support within the royal family. The Queen's response to these allegations was measured and conciliatory. She issued a statement expressing concern over the issues raised, particularly those of race, and emphasized that they would be addressed privately by the family. This response highlighted her attempt to manage the situation with sensitivity, acknowledging the seriousness of the issues while maintaining the family's privacy.

In both cases, Queen Elizabeth II's role was crucial in navigating the controversies. Her actions reflected a commitment to uphold the dignity and reputation of the monarchy. By balancing the need for public accountability and the preservation of the family's private matters, she navigated these challenges with a focus on the long-term stability of the monarchy.

These events have led to a gradual transition of responsibilities to the younger generation of royals.

Figures like Prince William and his wife Kate, along with Prince Charles, have increasingly taken on more prominent roles, preparing for the future succession and ensuring the continuity of the monarchy's public engagements and charitable work.

The COVID-19 pandemic also presented unprecedented challenges, and Queen Elizabeth II's leadership during this crisis was notable. She moved to Windsor Castle and observed strict sanitary protocols. Her televised addresses to the nation were moments of unity and reassurance. On April 5, 2020, her speech invoked a spirit of resilience and hope, reminiscent of the wartime addresses by her father, King George VI. Her ability to connect with the nation's sentiment, urging people to "never give up, never despair," was a poignant reminder of her role as a source of stability and comfort.

Despite the pandemic, the Queen maintained her commitment to public service. She attended the State Opening of Parliament, the G7 summit, and hosted US President Joe Biden, among other engagements. Her decision to award the George Cross to the NHS (National Health Service) acknowledged the tireless efforts of healthcare workers. Her use of a walking stick during public engagements and a brief hospital stay highlighted her vulnerability, yet her dedication to her duties remained unwavering.

The death of Prince Philip, Duke of Edinburgh, on April 9, 2021, after seventy- three years of marriage, marked the end of an era. The Queen, in her first moment of reigning as a widow, displayed profound resilience and dignity, particularly during Prince Philip's funeral, where COVID-19 restrictions necessitated her sitting alone, a moment that resonated with people around the world. Her personal tribute to her "beloved Philip" in her Christmas broadcast was a rare glimpse into her private sentiments, underscoring the depth of their partnership.

The Platinum Jubilee in 2022 celebrated seventy years of Queen Elizabeth II's reign, a historic milestone. The Jubilee was a testament to her longevity and dedication to public service. During this period, she met with several world leaders, including Canadian Prime Minister Justin Trudeau, and appointed her 15th British Prime Minister, Liz Truss. Her engagement in these significant political and public events, even amid personal health challenges, demonstrated her commitment to her constitutional duties.

Platinum Jubilee and Farewell

The year 2022 marked a historic moment in the British monarchy with the celebration of Queen Elizabeth II's Platinum Jubilee, followed by the solemn occasion of her passing. This period encapsulated both the celebration of a remarkable reign and the transition of the monarchy to a new era under King Charles III.

Queen Elizabeth II's Platinum Jubilee in February 2022 celebrated an unprecedented seventy years on the throne, a milestone no other British monarch had reached. The Jubilee was not just a commemoration of her accession but also a reflection on her extraordinary life and legacy. Her reign, spanning over seven decades, witnessed monumental changes in the world and the monarchy itself. Elizabeth II navigated these changes with a blend of tradition and modernity, earning respect and admiration from across the globe.

The Jubilee festivities were a nationwide celebration, marked by events that reflected the Queen's commitment to public service and the Commonwealth. However, the celebratory mood was tempered by her health challenges, which led to limited public appearances. Despite this, her presence, whether in person or in spirit, was a unifying force for the nation.

On September 8, 2022, Buckingham Palace announced concerns for the Queen's health. Later that day, the world received the news of her peaceful passing at Balmoral Castle at the age of ninety-six. Her death marked the end of an era and initiated the meticulously planned Operation London Bridge, outlining the protocol following the death of a monarch.

The nation and the Commonwealth entered a period of mourning, reflecting on the profound impact of her reign. Elizabeth's coffin was taken to St. Giles' Cathedral in Edinburgh, where thousands paid their respects. Her coffin was then flown to London, lying in state at Westminster Hall for four days. The public outpouring of grief was immense, with a quarter of a million people queuing for hours to pay their respects.

The state funeral, held on September 19 at Westminster Abbey, was a historic event, the first for a monarch since George II in 1760. It was attended by world leaders, dignitaries, and public figures, highlighting the Queen's global impact. The funeral procession and service were a blend of solemnity and pageantry, fitting for a monarch who had dedicated her life to her country and the Commonwealth.

In Windsor, a final procession took place, and poignant moments, such as her fell pony and two corgis standing at the side of the procession, symbolized the personal loss felt by many. Queen Elizabeth was laid to rest with Prince Philip in a private ceremony, bringing closure to their lifelong partnership.

The passing of Queen Elizabeth II heralded the beginning of King Charles III's reign. The transition to a new monarch brought both challenges and opportunities. King Charles III ascended the throne at a time of global uncertainty and faced the task of continuing the monarchy's relevance in a rapidly changing world.

Charles, having spent a lifetime preparing for this role, was expected to bring his own style to the monarchy. His long-standing commitment to environmental causes and social issues indicated a reign that would focus on contemporary global challenges. However, he also faced the delicate task of upholding the traditions and values that the monarchy represents, balancing modernization with the preservation of heritage.

Queen Elizabeth II's Platinum Jubilee and her subsequent passing marked a period of reflection and transition for the British monarchy. Her life and reign, characterized by devotion and adaptability, left a profound legacy that will influence the monarchy for generations to come. As King Charles III assumes the throne, he carries the responsibility of honoring this legacy while steering the monarchy into the future. The end of Elizabeth II's historic reign and the beginning of Charles III's era represent a significant chapter in the story of one of the world's oldest monarchies, symbolizing both continuity and change.

The Public Image and The Impact

In the pages of history, few monarchs have left an indelible mark quite like Queen Elizabeth II. Her reign, which began in the hopeful era following World War II, saw her transform from the enchanting "fairytale Queen" of the 1950s into a symbol of resilience, adaptability, and enduring grace. Her journey was not just a personal one; it was intertwined with the cultural and political evolution of Britain and its impact on the global stage.

The early years of Elizabeth's reign were characterized by a sense of optimism and rejuvenation. Post-war Britain looked towards a "new Elizabethan age," where progress and achievement were the orders of the day. Elizabeth, in her youth and vitality, embodied this spirit perfectly. She was glamorous and charismatic, captivating not only her subjects in the United Kingdom but people around the world.

However, every reign has its challenges. In 1957, Lord Altrincham's critique of her speaking style as reminiscent of a "priggish schoolgirl" marked one of the rare moments of public criticism she faced. This critique, however, did not dampen her spirit; instead, it catalyzed a shift towards a more modern monarchy. In the late 1960s, as aforementioned, this transition was evident through initiatives like the 'Royal Family' documentary and the televised investiture of Prince Charles as the Prince of Wales. These efforts demystified the royal experience, bringing the monarchy closer to the people.

Perhaps one of the most significant changes Queen Elizabeth II introduced was the 'royal walkabout.' This practice, initiated during a tour of Australia and New Zealand in 1970, allowed her to meet the public informally, breaking royal protocol and traditions. It was a revolutionary move, symbolizing a more accessible and less aloof monarchy. Her wardrobe, known for its solid-color overcoats and distinctive hats, was not just a fashion statement but a functional choice, ensuring she was visible in crowds.

The Silver Jubilee of 1977 was a testament to her popularity. The public's enthusiasm and the nationwide celebrations reflected the deep affection they held for their Queen. However, the following decade brought challenges as the royal family faced increased scrutiny, especially the personal lives of Elizabeth's children. The 1990s were particularly trying; public opinion wavered, and the Queen faced unprecedented criticism. In response, she adapted, opening Buckingham Palace to the public and agreeing to pay income tax – a move that showed her willingness to evolve with the times.

Despite these challenges, her popularity, especially during moments of national crisis, remained steadfast. The death of Diana, Princess of Wales, in 1997, was a critical moment. Elizabeth's address to the nation, a rare live television broadcast, was a pivotal point in reconnecting with the public, demonstrating her empathy and leadership.

Internationally, Queen Elizabeth II was immensely popular. This was evident in countries like Australia, where despite a republican movement, her personal charm and respect kept the monarchy intact. Leaders like Prime Minister Julia Gillard of Australia and Malcolm Turnbull, a former Australian republican movement leader, acknowledged her impact, with Turnbull notably saying, "She's been an extraordinary head of state."

Her influence was also reflected in public opinion polls. In 2006 and 2007, these polls showed strong support for the monarchy in Britain. During her Diamond Jubilee in 2012, her approval ratings soared to 90%. Even during the Platinum Jubilee and despite controversies surrounding the royal family, her personal popularity remained high, a testament to her enduring appeal and the respect she commanded.

Queen Elizabeth II was not just a monarch; she was a cultural icon, represented in various forms of media. Artists like Pietro Annigoni, Peter Blake, and Lucian Freud, and photographers such as Cecil Beaton and

Annie Leibovitz, captured her in their works, contributing to her enduring image.

While Queen Elizabeth's early years on the throne were characterized by a traditional approach to monarchy, as society evolved, so did she, subtly steering the royal institution through the waters of modernity. The 1960s and 1970s saw her embracing television as a means of connecting with her subjects, a significant departure from the radio broadcasts of her predecessors. The documentary 'Royal Family' and the televised investiture of Prince Charles were efforts to pull back the curtain on royal life, an attempt to resonate with a populace immersed in a rapidly changing world.

The introduction of the 'royal walkabout' during a tour of Australia and New Zealand in 1970 was a revolutionary step. It broke down barriers between the monarchy and the public, allowing for informal, personal interactions. This practice, now a staple of royal engagements, was emblematic of Elizabeth's subtle modernization of royal protocol.

The ever altruistic Queen supported over 600 organizations and charities as their patron. The Charities Aid Foundation calculated that, during her reign, Elizabeth contributed to raising more than £1.4 billion for these causes. She supported the British Red Cross, a prominent humanitarian organization aiding people in crisis both within the UK and globally. Her patronage also included The Royal British Legion, renowned for providing lifelong support to the British Armed Forces' members, veterans, and their families. Additionally, she championed Barnardo's, one of the UK's foremost children's charities, dedicated to aiding the nation's most vulnerable children and youth. Her support extended to Cancer Research UK as well, a pivotal organization focused on cancer prevention, diagnosis, and treatment. Furthermore, she was involved with Save the Children UK, which strives to enhance the lives of children through improved education, healthcare, and economic opportunities, along with providing emergency aid in various crises. The Royal National Lifeboat Institution (RNLI) also benefited from her patronage, an entity committed to saving lives at sea around the UK and Ireland's coasts. Her support was significant to The Duke of Edinburgh's Award, a program aimed at empowering young individuals, founded by her husband, Prince Philip. The Royal Society for the Prevention of Cruelty to Animals (RSPCA) was another beneficiary of her patronage, an organization dedicated to promoting animal welfare. The National Theatre, a leading performing arts venue, thrived under her patronage, committed to delivering world-class, engaging, challenging, and inspiring theater. Moreover, her support for The Scout Association underscored her commitment to the youth, an organization aimed at helping young people realize their full potential in various aspects of life.

Her numerous titles and honors reflected her status and the esteem in which she was held globally. In each of her realms, she held a unique title, from Queen of  Saint Lucia to Queen of Australia, each underscoring her role as a unifying figure. Her personal flag and royal cypher became symbols of her reign, recognized worldwide.

Elizabeth's lasting legacy is indelible and varied. It is found in her ability to adapt to changing times while maintaining the dignity and traditions of the monarchy. It lies in her unwavering sense of duty and commitment to public service. And perhaps most importantly, it is reflected in the deep affection and respect she garnered, not just in the United Kingdom but across the world.

Epilogue: A Queen Remembered

As the chapters of Queen Elizabeth II's reign close, we are left to reflect on the indelible mark she left not only on the British monarchy but on the world stage. Her life woven with threads of duty, resilience, and transformation, offers a narrative that transcends the mere passage of time. It is a story of a monarch who, with quiet strength and unwavering commitment, navigated the tides of change and stood as a beacon of continuity amidst a rapidly evolving world.

Queen Elizabeth II's reign, the longest in British history, was more than a chronological record of events; it was a journey of adaptability and perseverance. From the early days of her youth, marked by the echoes of war and the weight of an unexpected crown, to the twilight years of her reign, she embodied the essence of steadfastness. Her ability to embrace progress without losing sight of tradition allowed the monarchy to evolve, reflecting the changing face of the nation and the Commonwealth she so dearly cherished.

Her legacy is not confined to the grandeur of state occasions or the solemnity of her duties. It is found in the quiet moments - a smile shared with a young admirer, a comforting word in times of national sorrow, a look of understanding and empathy, a hand shaken with an AID's patient.

These moments, though fleeting, were threads in the fabric of her connection with people from all walks of life, making her not just a monarch but a cherished presence in the lives of many.

Over the years, Queen Elizabeth's fashion evolved into a signature style characterized by bright, block colors and matching hats - a pragmatic choice ensuring visibility in crowds. Her style became iconic, influencing trends and featured in exhibitions, demonstrating her impact on the fashion world.

As the baton is passed to a new generation, the story of Queen Elizabeth II's reign will continue to inspire and guide. It stands as a testament to the enduring relevance of the monarchy, its ability to adapt, and its unbreakable bond with the people it serves. The chapters may have concluded, but the narrative of her impact, her dedication, and her love for her nation and its people will continue to be told, echoing as a timeless legacy of a monarch who, with grace and fortitude, dedicated her life to her country and her people.

In the quiet after her reign, as the nation and the world reflect, it becomes clear that Queen Elizabeth II's story was not just about the crown she wore but about the lives she touched, the stability she provided, and the gentle strength with which she led. Her legacy, a blend of the past and the present, will continue to light the way into the future, a guiding star for the generations to come.

1. As a young child, Princess Elizabeth was showered with three tons of toys from foreign officials during her parents' tour. These gifts were generously distributed to hospitals and orphanages.

2 At the tender age of three, Hollywood tried to sign Princess Elizabeth, ultimately settling for Shirley Temple, a lookalike child star.

3 The Queen's mornings began at 7:30 am, listening to debates on the radio. Her baths were meticulously measured to be seven inches (approximately 17.8 centimeters) deep at 62 degrees Fahrenheit (about 16.7 degrees Celsius).

4. On her wedding day, Elizabeth's tiara broke, but the problem was quickly resolved as she had other tiaras to choose from. Elizabeth also listened to the BBC's live commentary of her wedding procession through speakers installed in her carriage.

5. Among her wedding presents was a hand-spun lace tray cover from Mahatma Gandhi, mistakenly thought by Queen Mary to be his dhoti (an Indian garment for lower body usually worn by Indian and South Asian men).

6. The Queen wasn't a fan of beards or mustaches, insisting Prince Philip shave his off after a naval tour.

7. To avoid needing the restroom during her nearly three-hour-long coronation ceremony, Elizabeth reportedly ate boiled eggs beforehand. Choirboys were given bread with peanut butter and Marmite for the same reason.

8. On coronation day, the Queen and The Duke of Edinburgh were driven from Buckingham Palace to Westminster Abbey in the Gold State Coach – pulled by eight grey gelding horses: Cunningham, Tovey, Noah, Tedder, Eisenhower, Snow White, Tipperary and McCreery.

9. The Coronation Bouquet was made up of white flowers – consisting of orchids and lilies-of-the-valley from England, stephanotis from Scotland, orchids from Wales, and carnations from Northern Ireland and the Isle of Man.

10. Since the Coronation, the Queen had worn the Coronation dress six times including the Opening of Parliament in New Zealand and Australia in 1954.

11. Elizabeth's breakfast typically included toast with a thin layer of butter, cereal from a yellow Tupperware container, and Darjeeling tea.

12. The royal dairy provided milk in bottles marked with the royal cypher E11R.

13. Over 300 billion postage stamps featured the Queen's image during her reign.

14. The Queen had specific food preferences, enjoying dark chocolate but avoiding garlic. She meticulously planned her meals and preferred her vegetables to be uniform in size.

15. After discovering a love for kippers (a dish made out of fish) during the war, the Queen learned to prepare them herself.

16. Elizabeth owned over thirty corgis throughout her life, starting with Susan. The 'Dorgi' breed was unintentionally created when one of her corgis mated with Princess Margaret's dachshund. Moreover, Elizabeth's love for her dogs was so great that a footman was demoted for inappropriately giving whisky to the Queen's corgis.

17. The palace staff was always prepared to clean up after the royal pets, discussing the challenges of pet care over tea with the Queen.

18. The Queen also personally penned plaques for her deceased corgis, burying them in a special graveyard at Sandringham.

19. Elizabeth bred black labradors and was involved in judging Kennel Club Retriever Trials.

20. The Queen's love for animals influenced her decision to replace a portrait of Queen Victoria with a painting of a dog at Windsor Castle.

21. By historical decree, the Queen owned all unmarked swans in open waters and 'fishes royal' in UK waters. She oversaw the annual Swan Upping count.

22. After enjoying Scotch pancakes at Balmoral, President Eisenhower received the recipe directly from the Queen.

23. The Queen enjoyed challenging jigsaw puzzles, a pastime present in all her residences.

24. The Queen often rode down Ascot racecourse early in the morning before official races commenced.

25. The Queen always had carrots on hand as treats for her horses.

26. The Queen played a key role in saving the Cleveland Bay horse breed from extinction in the 1960s.

27. In 1962, the Queen advised President Kennedy on managing Jackie's new horse.

28. Elizabeth only carried cash on Sundays to make church donations.

29. After it was revealed that the Queen stored her breakfast cereal in Tupperware, sales of the product increased dramatically.

30. During their visit to London after the Apollo 11 mission, astronauts Neil Armstrong, Buzz Aldrin, and Michael Collins met Queen Elizabeth II. Interestingly,

they presented her with a small piece of moon rock brought back from their historic lunar landing.

31. The Queen enjoyed imitating accents and personalities, including those of Margaret Thatcher and Boris Yeltsin.

32. During a Canadian visit in 1964, a flower, complete with roots and mud, accidentally hit the Queen when children were instructed to throw flowers at her car.

33. In 1981, the Queen awarded the George Cross to bodyguard Jim Beaton for his bravery in thwarting an attempted kidnapping of her in 1974. During the ceremony, she shared a light moment with Beaton's daughter.

34. Elizabeth danced with President Ford to 'The Lady Is A Tramp' during a 1976 White House visit, an event overshadowed by Elizabeth Taylor's presence the following day.

35. A 1979 Buckingham Palace event for the International Year of the Child featured Sir Cliff Richard and a choir. Smoke from torches caused disarray, but the Queen humorously took responsibility for trying to waft the smoke away.

36. During a ride with President Reagan, the Queen saved him from potential embarrassment by grabbing his horse's reins when he was distracted.

37. President Reagan gifted the Queen a computer during her 1981 visit to his California retreat, which she used for her horse-racing interests.

38. The Queen favored 'ballet slippers,' a pale pink shade of Essie nail polish.

39. In 1991, a podium mishap during a speech at the White House led to only the Queen's glasses and the top of her head being visible.

40. As the head of state, the Queen didn't need a passport or a driver's license. Every passport in the United Kingdom is issued with the monarch's name. As a consequence, Queen Elizabeth didn't need her own passport to travel.

41. Elizabeth enjoyed a gin and Dubonnet cocktail with ice and a slice of lemon, occasionally opting for a sweet German white wine instead.

42. The Queen used her handbag to discreetly communicate with her staff; its placement on the table or floor had specific meanings. If the Queen placed her handbag on the table at dinner, it signaled that she wanted the event to end in the next five minutes. If she placed her bag on the floor, it showed that she's not enjoying the conversation and wants to be rescued by her lady-in-waiting.

43. A 'brown bag' containing essential items like thick socks and clean gloves accompanied the Queen on her travels.

44. During a 2005 encounter with Eric Clapton at Buckingham Palace, the Queen inquired about the length of his music career.

45. During a state visit, a language barrier led to a humorous misunderstanding involving Madame de Gaulle's comment about retirement, swiftly clarified by the Queen.

46. President George W. Bush mistakenly added 200 years to the Queen's age during her 2007 visit to

Washington DC, prompting her to humorously reference the error in a later speech. Later, Michelle Obama unintentionally broke protocol by touching the Queen in 2011, but the Queen responded warmly, subtly reciprocating the gesture.

47. Artists found the Queen difficult to paint as she rarely sat still during portrait sessions.

48. The Queen's dislike for waste led her to discreetly donate second-hand outfits and wear some of her clothes for many years.

49. The Queen had a successful pigeon racing hobby, inheriting the royal pigeon loft from her father.

References

Anderson, Jodie. *The Queen's childhood and early years in photographs*. Good Housekeeping (2022). https://www.goodhousekeeping.com/uk/lifestyle/g40283855/queen-elizabeth-ii-childhood/ Accessed Feb 10, 2024.

Arbiter, Victoria. *Queen Elizabeth II: Monarch*. New York. Cavendish Square, 2017.

BBC Editors. *Queen Elizabeth II: Her life before she took the crown*. BBC (2022). https://www.bbc.com/news/newsbeat-62850275 Accessed Feb 15, 2024.

Bellini, Luciana. *Remembering Queen Elizabeth II, the Most Well-Traveled Monarch in History*. Condé Nast Traveler (2022). https://cntraveler.com/story/remembering-queen-elizabeth-ii-life-in-travel Accessed Feb 22, 2024.

Dougherty, Steve and Sutton, Larry. *QUEEN ELIZABETH II 1926-2022*. Everand (2022). https://www.everand.com/article/595090435/Queen-Elizabeth-Ii-1926-2022 Accessed Feb 20, 2024.

Grady, Constance. *The subtle power of Queen Elizabeth II's reign*. Vox (2022). https://www.vox.com/culture/2022/9/8/22846451/queen-elizabeth-ii-death-96-obituary-reign-monarchy Accessed Feb 18, 2024.

Hardman, Robert. *Queen of Our Times: The Life of Queen Elizabeth II*. London. Pegasus Books, 2022

Leduc, Sarah and Trouillard, Stéphanie. *Elizabeth II, a life on the throne*. France24 (2022). https://www.france24.com/en/europe/20220908-elizabeth-ii-a-life-on-the-throne Accessed Feb 25, 2024.

Loft, Philip. *70 Years: The Queen's role in the Commonwealth*. UK Parliament (2022). https://commonslibrary.parliament.uk/70-years-the-queens-role-in-the-commonwealth/ Accessed Feb 09, 2024.

Owen, James and Time Books. *The Times Queen Elizabeth II: A Portrait of Her 70-year Reign*. New York. HarperCollins Publishers, 2021

Walters, Meg. *The Story Of Queen Elizabeth II And Prince Philip's Relationship*. The List (2023). https://www.thelist.com/380722/the-story-of-queen-elizabeth-ii-and-prince-philips-relationship/ Accessed Feb 23, 2024.

Wilson, A. *The Queen: A Royal Celebration of the Life and Family of Queen Elizabeth II, on Her 90th Birthday*. London. Atlantic Books, 2023.

A Personal Note from Scott Matthews

 Stepping out from the shadows of authorship, I wish to connect with you on a more personal level. Crafting this book, *A Brief History of Queen Elizabeth II*, was a journey of deep passion and dedication, aimed at sharing the fascinating saga of Queen Elizabeth II's reign with you. Every chapter and narrative insight was designed to enrich your understanding and appreciation for her monumental legacy.

This work is not just a historical account; it represents a segment of my life devoted to exploring and celebrating the richness of royal history. The hours spent researching, the challenges encountered, and the bursts of inspiration—all were steps in this journey to bring history closer to you. Within these pages, I've included a photograph of myself in a moment of casual reflection, hoping to narrow the gap between us and offer you a glimpse into the life of the person behind the words.

Your reflections on this book hold immense value, both to me and to those who share our interest in royal histories. Reviews do more than support me as an author; they guide fellow enthusiasts to this story, helping to spread the knowledge and fascination with Queen Elizabeth II's era. I personally read every review, cherishing your insights and suggestions. The thought that my efforts might have touched you, or contributed to your historical journey, is incredibly fulfilling.

If this book has enlightened you, piqued your curiosity, or even if you see areas where it could be improved, I warmly invite you to share your perspective through a review. Please use the QR code provided below for convenience. Whether you're reading on a Kindle or holding a physical copy, a simple scan or click will let you share your thoughts.

Thank you for walking this historical path with me. Here's to a shared appreciation for history, and to the stories yet to be discovered.

Warm regards,

Scott Matthews

Find more of me on Amazon!

Check out the "Amazing Facts" series and learn more about the world around us!

Check out the "Why Do We Say That" series and learn where everyday idioms and phrases come from!

Made in the USA
Middletown, DE
21 March 2024

51889308R00062